PASTORAL
DYNAMO

PASTORAL DYNAMO

From the Perspective of

SAINT JOHN NEUMANN

FR. RICHARD BOEVER, CSsR

Liguori

Imprimi Potest: Stephen T. Rehrauer, CSsR, Provincial
Denver Province, the Redemptorists

Published by Liguori Publications, Liguori, Missouri 63057
Liguori Publications, a nonprofit corporation, is an apostolate of the Redemptorists
(Redemptorists.com).
To order, visit Liguori.org or call 800-325-9521.

ISBN 978-0-7648-2858-4

Cataloging-in-Publication Data is on file with the Library of Congress

Printed in the United States of America
26 25 24 23 22 / 5 4 3 2 1
First Edition

CONTENTS

Mon Journal I.

During his seminary years, John Neumann began recording his unguarded thoughts in what he called Mon Journal.

Foreword

FR. RICHARD BOEVER HAS WRITTEN a biography of St. John Neumann in the first person as if the saint were speaking to the reader. Fr. Boever's objective to focus on the humanity of St. John rather than on his accomplishments is achieved in an unusual way. The direct quotations of St. John throughout the text provide a moving context for the experiences of his life rooted in a deep trust in God.

This chronology of St. John Neumann's life includes the development of his deep faith from the early years until his death while bishop of Philadelphia. The reader is privileged to peer into his heart during his discernment of a priestly vocation and his perseverance in traveling across the Atlantic to the United States, where he was ordained.

Saint John's letters to his family in Bohemia are both tender and stirring in describing the challenges and joys of serving in the developing Church in the United States.

His life as missionary and bishop convey the holiness and humility that attracted so many souls to being disciples of Jesus Christ.

This book invites each of us to accompany St. John Neumann along his path of faithful discipleship, deepening our own commitment to discipleship and living out our unique vocation in Christ.

Cardinal Justin Rigali
Archbishop Emeritus of Philadelphia

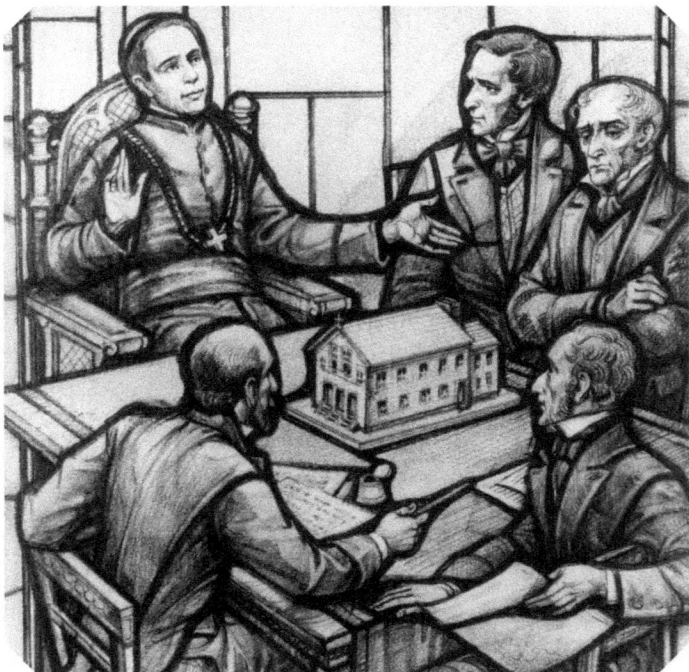

*A window at the National Shrine of St. John Neumann in
Philadelphia depicts the founding of the Catholic school system.*

Introduction

MUCH HAS BEEN WRITTEN ABOUT ST. JOHN NEUMANN (1811-50): his development of a school system, his dedication to the Eucharist and the Forty Hours devotion, plus his untiring energy in visiting distant places where his ministry was most needed. These are examples of his monumental accomplishments. In this book, my intention is not only to familiarize you with these enormous achievements but to also help you understand St. John as a person.

I began studying St. John Neumann while in search of material for my dissertation when I was a doctoral student at Saint Louis University. I knew the Redemptorists of the Baltimore Province were responsible for collecting primary sources about John Nepomucene Neumann, who had been canonized in 1977—the first American male to receive this honor. As I studied the life of St. John, I became interested enough to make his life and work the focus of my dissertation. Since then, I have remained "in contact" with St. John by praying with him, writing about him, and admiring him from across time. This latest adventure—the evolution of this book—has been a different experience.

A special thanks to the Redemptorists of the Baltimore Province who have preserved so much excellent material from the life of St. John Neumann and to the Redemptorists who read and commented on this book. Finally, thanks to the men and women of Liguori Publications for their attention to the many details of publishing this book.

"The merits of an active man are measured not so much in the number of deeds performed, as in his thoroughness and stability," Pope Benedict XV said of Neumann. "For true activity does not consist in mere noise. It is not the creature of a day, but it unfolds itself in the present. It is the fruit of the past and should be the good seed of the future. Are not these very characteristics the mark of the activity of Venerable Neumann? Bearing all this in mind, no one will any longer doubt that the simplicity of the works performed by our venerable servant of God did not hinder him from becoming a marvelous example of activity. Their very simplicity has forced us...to impress on our children...the proclamation of the heroic virtues of Neumann, since all find in the new hero an example not difficult to imitate."

Fr. Rich Boever, CSsR

Chronology

1811	Born and baptized, Prachatice, Bohemia (March 28)
1818	Elementary school
1823–29	*Gymnasium,* České Budějovice
1829–31	Philosophy level in České Budějovice
1831–33	Seminary studies in České Budějovice
1833–35	Seminary in Prague
1835	Completes studies (July 8), ordination delayed
1836	Sails to New York City (April 20–June 2)
1836	Ordained a priest, Diocese of New York (June 25)
1836	First Mass, St. Nicholas Church, New York City (June 26)
1836	Ministry in Buffalo (June 29–July 12)
1840	Joins Redemptorists (October 18)

1840	Redemptorist novice (November 30)
1842	Professes vows as a Redemptorist (January 16)
1844–47	Pastor and religious superior, St. Philomena, Pittsburgh
1847	Vicegerent of the Redemptorists in North America (February 9)
1849	Rector of St. Alphonsus Parish, Baltimore (January 9)
1852	Ordained bishop of Philadelphia (March 28)
1852	First meeting forming Catholic School Board (April 28)
1853	Forty Hours devotion inaugurated
1854	In Rome for the declaration of the Immaculate Conception (October 21)
1855	Visits loved ones in Bohemia (February)
1858	Exterior of Cathedral of Sts. Peter and Paul completed (September 13)
1859	Sisters of the Third Order of St. Francis begins
1860	Dies of apoplexy while on an errand, Philadelphia (January 5)
1963	Beatified by St. Paul VI
1977	Canonized by St. Paul VI

A List of Illustrations and Photographs

Page 6: As a seminarian, John Neumann began recording his unguarded thoughts in what he called *Mon Journal*.

Page 10: A window at the National Shrine of St. John Neumann in Philadelphia depicts the founding of the Catholic school system.

Page 18: In 1811, John Nepomucene Neumann was born in a house in Prachatice, Bohemia (now in the Czech Republic).

Page 20: John was the third of six children in his family.

Page 22: John attended a secondary school, or *gymnasium*, at České Budějovice, a day's journey from his hometown.

Page 26: At age 20, John continued his studies at the seminary in České Budějovice.

Page 29: While completing his seminary studies in the bustling city of Prague, John felt isolated and became deeply introspective.

Page 36: John's passport was used for travel within Europe, and eventually to the United States.

Page 40: As depicted in stained glass at the St. John Neumann shrine, John first set foot on American soil.

Page 44: Bishop John Dubois of the Diocese of New York ordained John Neumann a priest on June 25, 1836.

Page 52: Fr. Neumann had a friendly encounter with Indians while traveling alone through his 900-square-mile parish in Western New York.

Page 56: For nearly three years, Fr. Neumann was pastor of St. Philomena's Parish in Pittsburgh, serving there with Fr. Francis Xavier Seelos.

Page 61: Fr. Seelos and Fr. Neumann became close friends and roommates at St. Philomena.

Page 65: Fr. Neumann was sent to St. Alphonsus Church in Baltimore to recuperate from an illness. But days after his arrival, he was appointed superior of all the US Redemptorists.

Page 66: On March 28, 1852, Fr. Neumann was ordained as bishop of Philadelphia.

Page 69: When Bishop Neumann returned to visit his boyhood home, he was greeted by throngs of people with signs depicting his bishop's coat of arms.

Page 71: Bishop Neumann authored a catechism for German-speaking children.

Page 76: Bishop Neumann's passport as an American citizen is shown.

Page 80: Bishop Neumann supported establishing the Sisters of the Third Order of St. Francis, who began by serving in hospital ministry and developed into teaching schoolchildren.

Page 85: Bishop Neumann spurred construction of the Cathedral of Sts. Peter and Paul in Philadelphia.

Page 90: A rare portrait of Fr. John Neumann in his Redemptorist habit.

In 1811, John Nepomucene Neumann was born in this house in Prachatice, Bohemia (now in the Czech Republic).

CHAPTER 1

Early Life in Bohemia

THE TOWN OF PRACHATICE SEEMED to sprout from the ground with a beauty all its own. My presence made little difference to the Bohemian community [now part of the Czech Republic], but for me, this is where my roots began to grow. My parents were named Philip Neumann and Agnes Lebis. My father was a stocking weaver by trade who had immigrated from Bavaria, so we spoke German in our home. My mother was Czech, but I would not study that language until years later in the seminary. I was born on March 28, 1811, the third of six children. I was baptized that same day in the parish church and given the name of Bohemia's protector, St. John Nepomucene.

We were brought up in the old-fashioned school. Our parents were both deeply Christian. While our father supervised the five or six apprentices and workers in our home from morning to night, our mother never missed a

John Neumann was the third of six children in his family.

day hearing Mass, always taking along one of us children who was not yet in school. In my case, at times I needed the promise of a penny or something similar to coax me to go to Mass, rosary, and the Stations of the Cross.

At age seven, I entered the local elementary school and did well in my studies during my first six years of schooling. My love of books began in these early days—a love that tended to be an extravagance later in life, as I was often tempted to buy more books than I could afford. "I had acquired from my father...a decided passion for reading," I later wrote. "As a result, the time that others spent in sports or bird catching, I spent in reading all the books I could get hold of. This is the reason why my mother often called me 'the Little Bookworm.'"

From the days of childhood, I was taken by the wonders of nature that surrounded me. One night I was unable to sleep because I was so fascinated by the moon's ability to float in space without falling into the vast expanse of the universe. My mother told me to go to bed and let the moon float on its own. I began my study of botany in those days with the parish catechist in the church gardens. This interest continued into adulthood.

At age twelve, I finished my elementary studies in Prachatice and entered secondary school, or *gymnasium*, in České Budějovice, a day's journey from home. "Actually, I had very little studying to do," I wrote. "The catechist at home, during our few lessons each week, made us learn so much that with little preparation we could have been immediately promoted into the third class. That, however, was not permitted. I used the many idle hours and days in more and more reading—all kinds of books, whatever I could indiscriminately get my hands on."

In my third year at České Budějovice, however, I ran

John attended this secondary school, or gymnasium,
at České Budějovice, a day's journey from his hometown.

into a problem. We had a very old, good-natured professor who had an unfortunate addiction to liquor. As might be imagined, we made no progress in our studies. Eventually, the professor was dismissed from the school. His successor was as strict as he was learned, and he wanted us to crowd into six months the studies that should have been accomplished earlier under his predecessor. It came as no surprise that this accelerated schedule caused many students to fall behind in their studies.

In the years of gymnasium, I was also dissatisfied with the teacher of Christian doctrine. He was the personification of dryness and a stickler for verbatim recitations. So, the two hours of religious instruction were very irksome to me. At the end of my gymnasium school years, some of my grades were not as good as they could have been. Naturally, my father assumed I was finished with studies and that I was ready to exchange my books for a trade. It would have been appropriate timing to conclude my formal studies, and I even resolved to discontinue them. However, my family persuaded me to change my mind. I was allowed to take the final exam a second time and, after successfully passing it, I continued my studies.

During the two years of study following gymnasium, known as the school of philosophy, many changes took place within me and in my interests. At least a dozen students showed great aptitude for the sciences. We employed all our free time—even our days of recreation—communicating to one another about what we had learned. "During these two years I followed perhaps a little too much my inclination for the natural sciences," I later wrote. "Natural history, geography, physics, geology, astronomy kept me busy, while algebra, geometry, trigonometry, which I had formerly disliked, were now my favorite studies." I was less inclined toward some of the other subjects.

One day after a history test, my classmates saw me shaking my head. I explained I wanted to rid myself of the material I had just studied for the test. During my time as a student, I never abandoned my spiritual life. Within the course of study, I not only remained faithful to my prayers, but I also read and studied several works like *The Imitation of Christ* by Thomas à Kempis, and *The Sinner's Guide* by Venerable Louis of Granada. I did my best to practice virtue and avoid sin.

At the end of the philosophy years, the time came when I had to declare my field of future study. I cannot say that I was aware of any inclination toward the priesthood during my childhood. For one thing, the possibility of getting accepted into the seminary seemed slim—only twenty of the eighty to ninety applicants were accepted. Besides, I had great interest in the sciences, so my predisposition was to enter medicine.

While grappling with uncertainty about my choice of

a profession, I returned home during the autumn holiday that year. To my surprise, my father was not opposed to the idea of me going to Prague to study medicine, but my mother was saddened by the thought of my pursuit of this profession. I told her about my inability to procure recommendations from influential people for the study of theology, as I was not acquainted with anyone who would be able to make such a recommendation on my behalf.

She refused to listen to my reasoning and urged me to send a petition to the Episcopal Consistory. Honoring my mother's wishes, I drew up a petition for admission to the seminary and sent it by special messenger to the council. Without any recommendations and simply at my own request, I was admitted to the seminary. From that moment, the temptation to devote myself to the study of medicine disappeared. Without regret, I also gave up physics and astronomy almost entirely. I began my studies of the sacred science on November 1, 1831.

At age 20, John continued his studies at the seminary in České Budějovice.

CHAPTER 2

The Seminary

THE SEMINARY FOR THE DIOCESE WAS IN ČESKÉ BUDĚJOVICE, the town where—except for my earliest education in Prachatice—I had attended school until then. The small seminary had been established in 1804. I was happy there, surrounded by good friends and spiritual advisors. A good spirit prevailed among the professors, and with great ease they taught us much useful material in a short time. At the end of the first year of theology, I was one of the few allowed to receive the tonsure (ceremonial trimming of the hair on the crown of the head) and the four minor orders (specific ministries assigned to aspiring seminarians). These were signs of rapid, worthy progress toward the priesthood.

In the second year of theology, we had to study the New Testament in Latin and Greek, along with hermeneutics (biblical interpretation) and canon law. I found most interesting the epistles of St. Paul, which the professor expertly interpreted. About this time, I also began to read the publications of the Leopoldine Foundation, an organization established in Vienna to aid the Catholic missions in North America. I was especially interested in the letters of the Reverend Frederic Baraga and other missionaries working among the Germans in North America. Such publications spurred tremendous interest and led many to support the North American missions with prayers and donations.

In those days, I was profoundly influenced by these publications and by my studies of the missionary journeys of St. Paul. I found myself thinking more and more about the missionary life. I kept these thoughts to myself until I found out that one of my dearest friends was thinking along similar lines. In this way, there developed in one of my fellow students, Adalbert Schmid, and myself a sudden resolve to betake ourselves to North America as soon as we had attained our desired goal of ordination and had acquired some experience.

My decision to go to North America would require me to speak languages I had not yet mastered. I knew that English would certainly be necessary, and I was sure that being able to speak French also would come in handy. As it happened, each diocese was allowed to send two seminarians to the large seminary in Prague each year. For me, Prague was full of promise. I figured that Prague would provide me with more opportunities to learn these foreign

While completing his seminary studies in the bustling city of Prague, John felt isolated and became deeply introspective.

languages, so I contacted the Most Reverend Bishop of České Budějovice, Ernst Konstantin Ruzicka, and applied for one of these two positions. My request was granted, and I transferred to the much larger seminary in Prague for my last two years of seminary. Unfortunately, going to Prague was a difficult move for me.

During my years in Prague, I began writing my unguarded thoughts and feelings in what I called *Mon Journal*. The writings were not a diary as such but afforded me the opportunity to externalize my deepest longings, feelings, and frustrations. My entries often became a discussion of various issues with God, his Mother, or one of the saints. My journal served as a mirror for my beliefs and weaknesses. I wrote entries on most days while in Prague and continued to write in it during the years when I served as a parish priest in Western New York. During this time I tried unsuccessfully to find a spiritual director to help me navigate my course in life. Instead, I came to realize I would have to initiate my own dialogue with the Lord using my pen. With God's guidance, I would include only what would help me correct my faults and lead me to eternal life. So, keeping my journal was a kind of prayer, and a way to understand the movements of God in my life.

Before Prague, life seemed to unfold on its own, and all I had to do was to cooperate with the actions of God's grace as they emerged in my daily routine. But when I felt isolated in Prague and during the early years in the United States, I sank into an introspection that touched my tender conscience. In this state, I became ruthless in my thoughts. The trials I endured during that time led me to articulate what I truly believed about my life in God. "Oh, inexplicable labyrinth of life!" I wrote. "The Lord began to call me to himself by consolation; he put up with my deafness for three years, I turned to him halfheartedly. To what a beautiful way did the Lord point. He gave me milk because I could not have digested any other food. It was mother's milk, which strengthened me."

But in Prague, I came to learn a desolation that I now believe was required for me to grow in virtue. I found in myself an inclination toward self-doubt where I often felt unappreciated yet easily became vain when praised. Loneliness was especially difficult for me. I never realized how important my companions in the seminary at České Budějovice had been to me. So, when I experienced the isolation of Prague, it impacted me deeply:

Dear God, everybody is displeased with me. How can I evoke their affections? I am so fainthearted and timid!...Thinking about my friends today made me feel so disconsolate, especially after supper, that I started to cry! Here I am, with all my carelessness and indifference while my friends in

České Budějovice are surrounded by remarkable people and enjoy wise and holy spiritual direction! They don't even think of me anymore. In my loneliness and grief, they have forgotten all about me.

The lack of comfort from family or friends during my last two years of seminary and while working alone as a young priest in the wilds of New York affected me profoundly:

There is a terrible void in my soul, I am completely discouraged, I cannot pray. To whom shall I turn for help? Then arises an embittered spirit and hate against my Creator and Jesus in my soul. Pride and unbelief, animal and devilish desires want to engulf my tortured, abandoned soul. And to such blasphemous thoughts I feel a great inclination, despair offers me suicide as a desirable means to free myself from my torturing doubts, and this means even seems allowed because all regard for his phantom laws has left my soul.

I read the great spiritual authors seeking direction and counsel for my life and, though often inspired by these readings, they also made me all the more aware of the inadequacies in my own spiritual life. As the time for my ordination approached, my anxiety increased more with each passing day. What sort of a priest would I be with all my sinfulness, bad habits, inflexibility, stubbornness, and my host of spiritual and bodily frailties? "Lord, I am beginning to feel that awful state of depression coming over me again!" I wrote. "I lose all yen for prayer because you seem to have turned a deaf ear to my cries. My distress grows from day to day. My own weakness overwhelmed me, and I feared distance from God. My God, do not let this despair of mine continue. This faintheartedness and lack of faith is frightening."

I came to realize that my spiritual path was to be one of surrender:

I find peace. True, I feel but little devotion; my soul is dry and sluggish; but yet, O Lord Jesus, I believe in You, I hope in You, I love You, and I grieve for having ever offended You! Behold my resolution to live entirely for You, to be patient in sufferings, diligent in the fulfillment of my duties, humble before You and my neighbor, and devout in Your service. O my God, accept the sacrifice of my lowliness! Holy Immaculate Mother of my Jesus, pray for me, a poor sinner, that I may worthily receive my God!

My decision to go to Prague grew out of a desire to prepare for a missionary life in North America. I wanted to learn and practice English. But to my dismay, when I arrived at the Prague seminary, I found out that English was not taught at the university and classes in French were forbidden by the archbishop. So much in the French Church seemed contrary to his theology that he even forbade the study of their language. I resolved to do the best I could in this situation. I would learn languages on my own. I supplemented my private language studies by conversing in English with some factory workers I met in the city. I also studied French on my own and began writing in *Mon Journal* in three languages—English, French, and German—just for the practice. During this time, I also continued to develop my familiarity with Italian by translating *The Way of Salvation and Perfection* by St. Alphonsus Liguori. I read the works of St. Teresa of Ávila and the letters of St. Francis Xavier in Spanish. In addition, I learned Greek, Latin, and Hebrew, as they were required for scriptural studies in the seminary.

As my seminary time drew to a close, our class received sad news. After all the preparation for missionary life and the priesthood, we found out we would not be ordained at the end of our seminary studies. We were informed that there would be no ordinations in my Diocese of České Budějovice because no new priests were needed. The diocese already had a sufficient number of clergy. I had not yet approached an American bishop seeking ordination because my original plans involved ordination in Bohemia with my family present, with the start of my missionary work after a time. My family did not know then of my desire to go abroad.

John's passport was used for travel within Europe, and eventually to the United States.

CHAPTER 3

Departure from Home

IN JULY OF 1835, after my time at the seminary in České Budějovice when normally I would have received the sacrament of holy orders, I returned home. I remained firm in my resolve to emigrate to the United States but still anticipated that ordinations would be scheduled before I left Bohemia. After three weeks at home, I finally found the courage to tell my parents and other family members about my intention to go abroad as a missionary.

Having told my family of my plans to be a missionary, I began to prepare for the journey. It took some time to get a passport which would allow me to emigrate from Bohemia. I was granted one in December. After eight months passed without a scheduled ordination for my class, I realized I had to make a move to get on with my life. Even though there was no reply from any of the bishops I had written about my offer to go to the United States, I knew I would have to make my journey anyway and trust in divine providence.

On February 8, 1836, I finally left home and began my travels across Europe. I could not say goodbye to my family face to face. It was simply too hard for me, and I knew it would be too difficult for them. "Ah, my Jesus, you must tear my heart from this world that it may be healed!" I wrote. "O Jesus, be my Savior!"

After visiting with the bishop, who was reluctant to lose me to a foreign land, I traveled through the snow-covered Bohemian Forest. I arrived in Munich on February 20, where I visited my cousin, Philip Janson, and I met Fr. John Martin Henni, who was already a missionary in Cincinnati and who would later become the bishop of Milwaukee. He told me it was unwise to sail to the United States without word from one of the bishops regarding open ministry positions. What was I to do? It took a long time to send and receive communications, and I did not have enough money to remain at home. I continued to Strasbourg, France, by way of Augsburg, Bavaria. Since my means were slim, I was encouraged to go to Paris and await a reply from one of the American bishops. My future now seemed all the more uncertain. Even so, I wrote: "But no evil shall befall me, for I am yours, my Jesus, and you are mine! Men cannot injure me, for you are omnipotent!"

By March 22, I was almost 200 miles away from home. My purse had dwindled to one hundred twenty-five francs, with no promise of financial help from other sources. My birthday fell on Palm Sunday that year. I was twenty-five years old and spent Holy Week in prayer in France and celebrated Easter. Eventually, I knew I could no longer wait for a letter from an American bishop, so on the Tuesday after Easter, I journeyed to the harbor for the final part of my voyage to America. I arrived in Le Havre on April 7, 1836. After a visit to the Blessed Sacrament, I got my first glimpse of the Atlantic Ocean. It was exactly as I had imagined it.

The next day, I found the ship *Europa*, securing a second-class ticket for the April 12 sailing date. However, we did not sail until April 20. It had been a long journey across land from Prachatice to this harbor, and I was about to commence another forty-day journey at sea. As I boarded the ship, I was filled with so many feelings—the sadness of leaving home, the anxiety over what waited ahead. I knew that, when I arrived in New York, I had neither an address to find nor any person to meet me and show me the way. I was on a journey that would take me to a new life.

Few Bohemians considered missionary life in the United States in the early 1800s. But what I found especially difficult about leaving the Old World was the unknown that awaited me in New York. The *Europa* was a nice enough ship. It had three masts, and it was 210 feet long. There was one passenger for each foot in length of the ship. Needless to say, there was not much privacy, and at times I was quite repulsed by the manners and scurrilous talk among some

John first sets foot on American soil, as depicted in stained glass at the St. John Neumann shrine.

of my fellow emigrants. Some of these passengers mocked my piety, so I kept to myself. Because I was quite unskilled in conversation about daily events, I journaled in Latin to discourage curious eyes. I also read from *The Imitation of Christ* by Thomas à Kempis and *An Introduction to the Devout Life* by St. Francis de Sales. The trip was a long forty days, but like Christ in the desert before his ministry began, I thought of the voyage as a gift from God. All things considered, my journey passed very well.

Then at last, early on the vigil of Trinity Sunday, May 28, 1836, I wrote: "We sighted America in a fine mist, and on Sunday evening we anchored at quarantine about one hour from Staten Island. It is indescribable how good it is for human eyes when one sees land again after wandering about for forty days. All who could only stand on their feet a little came and as if by magic lost all sickness and weakness. There was no end to the rejoicing and singing."

I had one dollar in my pocket on the day I finally touched shore after the required quarantine. Nonetheless, I was filled with such joy that it did not concern me. I came to the United States to be a priest, a missionary. Still, I breathed a sigh of relief and said a prayer of gratitude once I stepped on shore.

My first care was to find a Catholic church. I walked along the mile-long streets of the city until evening. I found a large number of churches, chapels, etc., but no Catholic church wanted to show itself. I had to put all my philological knowledge together to explain to myself from the inscriptions of these buildings, often decorated with ideal beauty, whether and in which Christ they believed....Now that I am here, all uncertainty has disappeared. I see the goal of my wishes, the dear aim of my resolutions before me. Quietly and naturally you, my Jesus, untie the knot which seemed to me too intricate.

I had one dollar in my pocket on the day I finally touched shore after the required quarantine. Nonetheless, I was filled with such joy that it did not concern me. I came to the United States to be a priest, a missionary. Still, I breathed a sigh of relief and said a prayer of gratitude once I stepped on shore.

Bishop John Dubois of the Diocese of New York ordained John a priest on June 25, 1836.

CHAPTER 4

Priest of the Diocese of New York

———————————

THE CITY OF NEW YORK IN 1836 NUMBERED 300,000 INHABITANTS and stretched along Broadway about one mile from the Battery to Twenty-Fifth Street, which was in the countryside. Most of the city's population was below Fourteenth Street. I walked down endless blocks in the rain all day. It was a good thing that I was already accustomed to walking long distances at a quick pace, but by the end of the first day, I still had not satisfied my quest. I had not found a Catholic church. I was finally given directions to the cathedral, where it so happened a German-speaking priest resided with the bishop. He greeted me like a long-lost brother. As it turned out, my anxiety about finding a welcoming diocese was unnecessary. A letter had been sent to Europe three weeks earlier saying that I had been accepted into the Diocese of New York! Since I had already set sail by the time the letter was sent, I did not receive the correspondence. When I finally met Bishop John Dubois, he informed me I would be ordained as soon as he returned from a pastoral visit to a remote area of the diocese. What a wonderful bishop! On June 25, 1836, Bishop Dubois ordained me a priest in Old St. Patrick's Cathedral. My ordination had the simplicity of Jesus' presentation in the Temple, though the Catholic paper included the event with a few lines, misspelling my name "Father John Newman." But to me, the ceremony was glorious. It was the event that marked the beginning of a new life that I felt confident was providentially directed by God.

My first and only assignment as a diocesan priest of New York would take me to the region between Lakes Ontario and Erie, near Niagara Falls. In that location were several German congregations north of Buffalo, about 500 miles west of New York City. Along the way, in Rochester, there was a German-speaking community in the process of forming and building the parish of St. Joseph. They were delighted to have a priest who spoke their language, and Bishop Dubois instructed me to spend some time with them. I immediately began teaching catechism to the young people. Some of the people wanted me to remain in Rochester so I could minister to the needs of the parish, but the arrival of Fr. Joseph Prost, CSsR, and other Redemptorists who were to take charge of the parish made it possible for me to continue to Buffalo. I was very impressed by the Redemptorist priest and his colleagues.

Twenty years prior to my arrival in America, there were few Catholics in the United States. As a result, not much attention was paid to them. But during my years there, 4.37 million immigrants came to that nation, and nearly 1.5 million of those spoke German. For these immigrants who were often isolated because of language and culture, the Church became the center of their social lives.

Fr. Alexander Pax, the resident pastor in Buffalo, was overjoyed to see me. Because he had been the only priest working in that region at the time, he was near exhaustion. He offered me the more settled parish in Buffalo, but I decided to take the outlying area under my wing. I traveled eight miles northeast of Buffalo to Williamsville, which had the beginnings of a stone church—still without a roof. The town was centrally located in the region where I would begin my ministry. The town had a settlement of four houses, and I took up residence with a Catholic family there. My new parish radiated out from this central church about fifteen miles, encompassing a 900-square-mile area. There were 400 Catholic families, and of these, 300 spoke German. The parish included the communities of North Bush, Lancaster, and eventually the towns of Transit, Sheldon,

Batavia, Pendleton, and Towanda. My nearest out-mission was two hours away, and the farthest was twelve. I wrote home about my early experiences:

> For the most part, the children had not been in any school, know German badly, English just as badly; besides that, they very seldom have an idea of the supernatural world....Like an old German emperor followed everywhere by his court, do I carry with me all needful church articles when visiting my three parishes of Williamsville, North Bush, and Lancaster. From an American citizen here I have received two acres of land for a church. I lived at North Bush with a native of Lorraine who, in consideration of payment in his next life, furnishes me with board and lodging. My furniture consists of four chairs lately purchased with some money I had laid by, two trunks, and a few books. For your consolation, I will tell you that the timber for my future residence has already been cut, and my people are rejoicing in the prospect of supplying me with corn, potatoes, etc. I have never yet suffered from hunger; and as for clothes—when one garment grows too shabby for wear, someone or other of my good people provides me with another....What joy would be

yours could you see the affection entertained for me by my good parishioners; and again would you rejoice at the sight of our holy religion planted and cultivated, with the help of divine grace, in the midst of these dark forests.

In the forests that I had to roam while going from one parish to another, I was intrigued by the vegetation I noted as I walked. I always had a keen interest in botany, and these journeys afforded me a wonderful opportunity to gather specimens of flora that was not known back in Bohemia....In the forests, beech, oak, ash, and linden trees abound, and in some places are also found the finest cedars. The sugar maple provides the sugar in ordinary use here....Apple, pear, and cherry trees succeed here very well, but they are all young; the land has been cultivated only during recent years....A species of insect, which they call mosquitoes, bite producing a violent swelling and causes the greatest suffering to both man and beast. Even during the sermon, I must constantly use my handkerchief to drive them off. The plants and flowers here are for the most part strange, but very beautiful. Lilies grow wild in the woods, as do likewise red currants, gooseberries, raspberries, and bromberry....Of the birds known at home, I found only the crows and night owls; the other kinds seen here are much more beautiful, but rarely have I heard any of them sing. There were bears and wolves in this neighborhood until quite recently, but it seems now they have been entirely exterminated by the Indians who still roam the forests here....Quite common are the beautiful skunks, whose odor is so dreadful that the stench of a decaying animal compared to it is incense. The rabbits are smaller, more rare, and in winter they are snow white. Poisonous rattlesnakes are still sometimes met with, but the Indians have shown the immigrants different plants which counteract their bite. Among the very commonly occurring poisonous plants there are especially two species which are so dangerous that they cause painful swelling of the members in persons of weak constitutions even without coming in contact with them. These plants are called *Toxicodendron radicans*. The weather here is very changeable; rarely does it rain, fair weather, heat or cold last longer than three or four days together. The place from which I am writing you these lines lies between Lake Ontario and Lake Erie and is somewhat more healthy by reason of the continual wind. These two lakes, like all the others in North America, contain the purest fresh water. These lakes likewise abound in fish, a matter of great advantage to those who live here.

Ministering in my parishes among people of various nationalities, I noticed the cultural differences among these immigrants—particularly between the Irish and the Germans. By the grace of God, these distinctions did not cause religious division in the Church. These differences were cultural rather than matters of doctrinal teachings. The handbook of all Catholics is the catechism, which transcends national borders.

There were times when I was uncomfortable walking through the woods. On one occasion while on a ministerial visit, I decided to stop and rest on a fallen tree trunk. I noticed shadows nearby but could not discern what they might be. Eventually, I realized I was being observed by a band of roving Indians. I prayed, but when the Indians found out that I was a "black robe," they spread out a buffalo skin and carried me to my destination. Another time, I was confronted and ordered to stop by a drunken man with a pistol. I continued walking without a word. By the grace of God, I am still alive. Still another time, I got lost. It was terribly frightening to be lost in the woods in an area where no one lives. Getting lost like that could mean

Fr. Neumann had a friendly encounter with Indians while traveling alone through his 900-square-mile parish in Western New York.

death. As it turned out, it meant that I was able to help one of my parishioners. I came upon an Irish settler deep in the woods. He was quite sick, and I was able to revive him with my altar wine. Eventually, the man recovered and told me how to get to my desired destination. He never forgot the encounter, and neither did I.

One problem I discovered soon after my arrival were the trustees who caused tribulations for me and others throughout my ministry. In the United States, the Catholic Church was not allowed to own property as its own entity. It was not recognized as an institution, so the parish itself could not own property. As a result, leaders in parish communities had to become owners of church properties. These trustees sometimes got "too big for their britches," as they say here, and tried to control things that were beyond their expertise. Outside of the Catholic community itself, there existed an anti-Catholic and anti-immigrant sentiment in the population. The great influx of so many Catholic immigrants was changing the ethnic makeup of the population of the country and the resulting land ownership. Harassment of Catholics happened everywhere, and many incidents occurred in which the perpetrators were never found. These kinds of antagonists eventually formed a political party called the Know-Nothings because no one owned up to their prejudiced actions.

To my great delight, Wenzel, my younger brother,

joined me in New York in 1839. He took me by surprise two days before the feast of his holy patron, St. Wenceslaus. The good news and loving messages he brought me dispelled all uneasiness and carried me back home in my imaginings. He was a godsend and acclimated quickly to his new surroundings. "In my absence, he conducts the German Catholic school for the parish in North Bush," I wrote. "For the rest, he is also cook, housekeeper, and stable boy. It is already much easier for me to fulfill my mission duties." In time, Wenzel would follow me into the Redemptorists as a Brother of great reputation.

The matter of vocation is mysterious, and if I tried to explain some of my own happenings, they would probably not make sense. When I was still in the seminary in Prague, and after I decided to become a missionary in North America, I jotted a thought in my journal that perhaps I should consider joining the Jesuits or the Redemptorists. It was just a passing thought at that time and not a serious consideration. The reason for the initial thought stemmed from the fact that I knew both communities had missionaries in North America, and at the time, I was still concerned about how I was going to fulfill my dream.

Later, I had written to Fr. Joseph Prost, a Redemptorist, about the regulations for bestowing the scapular on a person. He gave me the answer but also wrote a cryptic line that touched me: *Vae Solis*. That is "Beware of the solitary life." The words echoed in my mind because I was experiencing the difficulties of this life on the frontier of Western New York. In the context of my spiritual aridity, I considered the words of Fr. Prost and eventually resolved to do something about my experiences. I decided to become a Redemptorist:

> For four years now I had spared myself no pain to bring the parishes under my care to fervor similar to that which I had observed at St. Joseph's Parish in Rochester. But things would not go that way. This, as well as a natural, or rather supernatural desire to live in a community of priests where I would not have to be exposed alone to the thousand dangers of the world made me suddenly resolved to request from Father Prost...admittance into the Congregation of the Most Holy Redeemer...and received from him acceptance in a letter of the 16th of September from Baltimore.

When I finally left the Diocese of New York to join the Redemptorists, my brother, young Wenzel, stayed behind and gathered our things. I arrived in Pittsburgh on October 18, 1840, followed by Wenceslaus in November that same year. We both entered the Redemptorists—I as a priest and Wenzel as a religious brother.

For nearly three years, Fr. Neumann was pastor of St. Philomena's Parish in Pittsburgh, serving there with Fr. Francis Xavier Seelos.

CHAPTER 5

Redemptorist Years

THE SONS OF ST. ALPHONSUS LIGUORI FIRST GATHERED IN 1732 IN NAPLES, ITALY. That was one hundred years before the first Redemptorist missionaries arrived in North America in 1832. The Redemptorist vicar general in Vienna, Fr. Joseph Passerat, sent three priests and three religious brothers to start a ministry in America that year. From then until now, the order has set deep roots in the United States.

I had the distinction of being the first person invested with the Redemptorist habit in America. That took place on November 30, 1841, when Fr. Prost—the superior of the Redemptorists in North America—came to Pittsburgh for that purpose. There was no established norm for how a novitiate period should be conducted in America. One thing was certain: there were too few priests and too much work to consider having an ordained person like myself not involved in apostolic work—even during the novitiate year.

On my first day in my Redemptorist habit, I was given the high Mass to sing in the church. Other assignments followed, one after another: "I daily made two meditations and two examens of conscience with the community, spiritual reading in private, and a visit to the Blessed Sacrament," I wrote. "I recited the rosary also, and that was all."

There was just too much apostolic work that needed attention. "My reality was that I just wasn't to have the year of prayer and reflection normally associated with a novitiate," I wrote. On December 8, 1841, I arrived in Baltimore and was granted a bit more than a month for quiet and solitude until I made my profession of vows as a religious on January 16, 1842. I was the first Redemptorist to profess his vows in the United States. The Redemptorists would continue to increase in number. My first assignment as a professed Redemptorist was as an assistant priest at St. James Parish in Baltimore. The parish was entrusted to the Redemptorists by Bishop Samuel Eccleston when the old St. John's Church, where we had been, was torn down to make way for St. Alphonsus Church. Saint Alphonsus became known as the German cathedral. Most of the time, there was only one priest at home at a time. The others usually were traveling to minister to surrounding German communities. These missions included East Hartford, Shrewsbury, and Frederick in Maryland; York and Cumberland in Pennsylvania; and Richmond in Virginia. There was no shortage of need for our ministry among the German-speaking immigrants. Still, it was a blessing to pray with members of the community and to work so closely with them as often as possible.

With donations from the Leopoldine Foundation (an organization established to aid Catholic missions in North America), the construction of St. Alphonsus Church got under way. Construction of another large Redemptorist church, St. Philomena in Pittsburgh, was also progressing but without the liberal contributions from Europe. Due to the lack of funds, construction at St. Philomena was slower than at St. Alphonsus. The vicegerent appointed to administer these projects was not pleased with the slow progress in Pittsburgh. So, in March 1844, I was sent to that city to move things along.

The Diocese of Pittsburgh was split off from the Diocese of Philadelphia eight months before my assignment there. Bishop Michael O'Connor was the first bishop of the Pittsburgh diocese. There were 6,000 German immigrants in Pittsburgh—even more in the surrounding area. Despite the large number of German Catholics in the area, St. Philomena Parish was short of money, with a large debt accruing during the church construction. In fact, the walls of the church were only half built when I arrived. I could do little more than establish a Church Building Society, asking each parishioner to contribute at least a nickel each week toward the construction. Later, Bishop O'Connor would claim that I had built the church without money! Little did he know how much anxiety this project caused me.

The real glory of St. Philomena was not the construction of the church itself, but the devotion the parishioners demonstrated throughout the process. For this, I credit the extraordinary men who were stationed with me at St. Philomena. My confrere, Fr. Francis Xavier Seelos, was especially outstanding. He certainly exhibited the zeal and the holiness of his namesake. Living with him was a blessing. We shared a room in the rectory, with only a curtain separating our sleeping areas. Our entire community was full of dedication and devotion. The community spirit among us inspired the same among the parishioners. Confraternities and pious societies were established that helped increase the bonds among parishioners, thus strengthening the parish. The parish school also thrived. Our pastoral focus at St. Philomena's included the surrounding countryside and, as a result, the communities we served eventually grew into fifteen separate parishes.

Unfortunately, I never seemed to have enough strength to do the work I wanted to do. I managed to develop a catechism for teaching the children and a Bible history for teaching them salvation history. These works proved to be very popular among the German-speaking clergy over the years in their efforts to catechize parishioners. One day,

Fr. Francis Xavier Seelos (above), beatified in 2000, and Fr. Neumann became close friends and roommates at St. Philomena.

my confreres, after observing me coughing blood, grew worried about my health. They wrote of their concern to our superior in Baltimore, Fr. Peter Czackert. He ordered me to see a doctor, who subsequently gave a negative report about the state of my health. I was ordered back to Baltimore where I was to be relieved of the various offices I held in Pittsburgh. I was actually delighted with the idea of being an assistant pastor while recuperating. Things, however, did not work out as anticipated.

I was at St. Alphonsus Parish but a few days when I received a message that totally surprised me. I was appointed superior of all the Redemptorists in the United States! This was incomprehensible to me. The superiors from Europe had come to study the progress of the Redemptorists in North America in 1845 and, in four months, they had visited all of the American houses. The provincial concluded that the rapid expansion of the Redemptorists that began early in the decade had to be slowed. It was clear that the confreres were overwhelmed with work, and a large debt had accrued due to the construction of so many new churches. When I was put in charge of the men in America, I had been a Redemptorist for only five years. I was charged with retrenching and slowing down our expansion.

My primary objective in my new position as the vicegerent was to make sure that the provincial's regulations and plans were carried out in the United States. I was confident this was what obedience demanded of me. Obviously, not all the men in America agreed with the Belgian provincial. Many believed the Redemptorists could not afford to stop expansion in the United States due to the dire needs of the immigrants for our help. I understood their concerns and appreciated their zeal. Yet, I did not feel I had the freedom to chart that course for our mission. The direction had been given by higher authority, and I was simply appointed to implement the directives given from Europe. We Redemptorists had ten communities in the United States at the time. These were mostly located in large urban areas, and from these houses the priests and brothers served seventy out-missions.

I sometimes think my greatest accomplishment during my time as superior was not so much in the work I was able to do within my own community but in the way I was able to help the women religious who were so vital to Church life in the United States. In the summer of 1847, the School Sisters of Notre Dame arrived from Munich. I first offered Mother Theresa Gerhardinger a building attached to St. James Parish that originally was used to house the Redemptorist novices. Before long, the sisters were teaching in all three of our German-speaking parishes in Baltimore. The Oblate Sisters of Providence was another community of sisters that stole my heart. From their beginnings in 1828, they cared for children of color. Unfortunately, by 1847 the new archbishop had no one to serve as chaplain for the Oblate Sisters and, as a result, he was on the verge of disbanding the community. I had to do something, so I sent one of our greatest men, Fr. Thaddeus Anwander, to talk to the bishop. While I was at home praying for his success, Fr. Anwander was on his knees, begging the bishop not to disband the community. Ultimately, the bishop agreed.

In 1847, the American houses were moved from the jurisdiction of the Belgian provincial and placed under the authority of the Austrian provincial. His philosophy about ministry in the United States differed from our former superior. He allowed us to accept the new foundations of Detroit and New Orleans—contrary to directions originally set by the Belgian provincial. In time, my term of office as superior of the Redemptorists in the United States ended, and the responsibility was assigned to another man. I was finally able to return to the ordinary apostolic labors of hearing confessions, preaching, visiting the sick, and teaching the children of St. Alphonsus Parish. "How good it is to be in the Congregation and to live in America," I wrote. "Here we can truly love God, work much, and suffer a lot for him, and we do all this quietly and unnoticed by the world."

Fr. Neumann was sent to St. Alphonsus Church in Baltimore to recuperate from an illness. But days after his arrival, he was appointed superior of all the US Redemptorists.

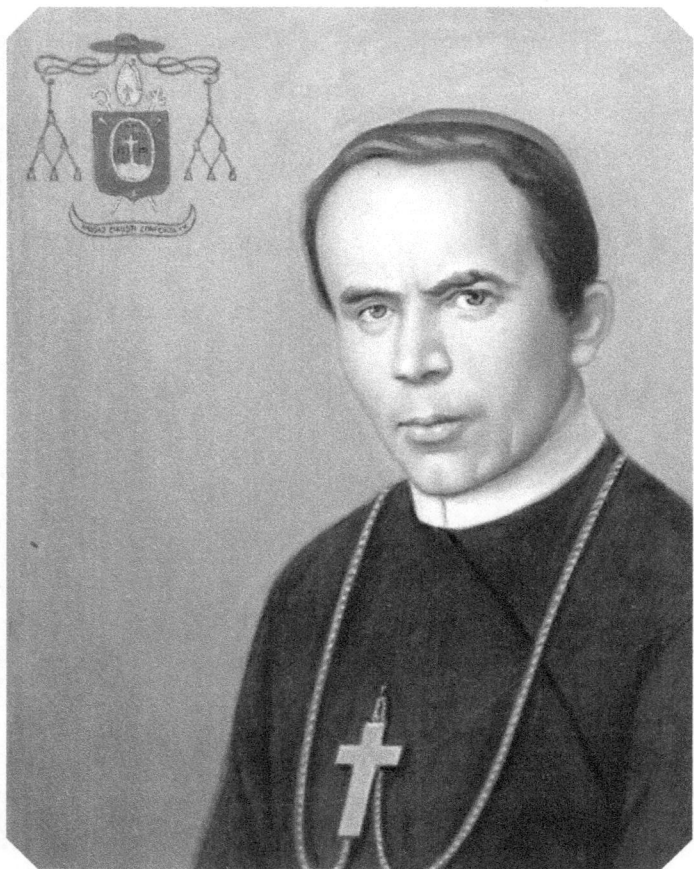

On March 28, 1852, Fr. Neumann was ordained as the fourth bishop of Philadelphia.

CHAPTER 6

Bishop of Philadelphia

ONE DAY UPON RETURNING HOME TO THE RECTORY OF ST. ALPHONSUS AFTER AN ERRAND, I spotted a pectoral cross and a ring on my bedroom dresser. I asked who had been in my room and was told that Archbishop Peter Kenrick had shown up for his regular confession. Oh, sweet Lord! I fell to my knees in prayer. In recent months, while I was busy about my ordinary apostolic endeavors, the bishops of the United States were writing back and forth, surfacing names so that Archbishop Kenrick could propose to Rome worthy candidates for the bishopric of Philadelphia. Three names eventually were sent to Pope Pius IX as candidates for the position of the fourth bishop of Philadelphia. Although I was second on the list, the Holy Father chose me as the new bishop. He made the appointment, requiring that I obediently accept the position without appeal.

Philadelphia was considered the United States' cradle

of freedom. A prosperous, elegant society had emerged in that city, and the people there would expect a bishop who was able to mingle with them with ease. The diocese itself was very large. It spanned more than 35,000 square miles and included half of Pennsylvania, all of Delaware, and a good portion of New Jersey. There were 170,000 Catholics in the diocese then, along with 113 parishes and 100 priests. Nativists and the Know-Nothing Party, with their anti-Catholic sentiments, had a strong presence in the city. I was certain my foreign accent would confirm their prejudiced belief that the papists were trying to take over the United States by sending millions of immigrants to America. I was not quite forty-one years old.

I chose my episcopal motto from the Anima Christi: *Passio Christi, conforta me!* which means "Passion of Christ, strengthen me." On the day before my ordination to the bishopric, Fr. Bernard Hafkenscheid, the vice provincial of the American Redemptorists, ordered me to pen my autobiography, which I did for the Redemptorists. I told one of the confreres that night: "If our Lord gave me the choice either to die or to accept this dignity, I should prefer to lay down my life tomorrow rather than be consecrated bishop; for my salvation would be more secure at the judgment seat of God than it will be if I appear before it burdened with the responsibility of a bishopric."

On my forty-first birthday—Passion Sunday, March 28,

When Bishop Neumann returned to visit his boyhood home, he was greeted by throngs of people with signs depicting his bishop's coat of arms.

1852—I was consecrated the fourth bishop of Philadelphia by Archbishop Kenrick. When all was prepared and I was dressed in bishop's colors, I told the confreres: "The Church treats her bishops like a mother treats a child. When she wants to place a burden on him, she gives him new clothes."

My mission as the bishop of this immense diocese began immediately. In the first week, I conferred the sacrament of confirmation six times, preaching at each occasion. I wrote my first pastoral letter fewer than ten days after arriving in Philadelphia. I believed it was important to ask for the people's support and prayer. Four weeks later, I sent a circular letter to all the clergy to spur on construction of our unfinished Cathedral of Sts. Peter and Paul. I stated theological positions on learning in a lecture to the Philopatrian Institute, a Catholic literary society. I told them that all pursuit of knowledge should further the interest of God and be used in his service. From the beginning, I was a busy bishop without a support staff. As I told my relatives back home: "A bishop in America has to do everything himself and by his own hand."

Less than two months after I became bishop in Philadelphia, I was back in Baltimore for the First Plenary Council of Baltimore. All the bishops of the United States assembled for the first time in plenary session to consolidate the legislation and practices of Catholic life in America. During the session, the bishops addressed many topics and issues—trustees, parish schools, liturgical practices, immigration, the need to reduce the size of some larger dioceses, and the establishment of financial and administrative guidelines. I served on two committees: one that examined liturgical ceremonies and another that addressed

Kleiner

Katechismus.

Verfaßt

von

Johann Nep. Neumann,

Bischof von Philadelphia.

J.S. M

Zehnte Auflage.

Mit

Genehmigung des National-Concilium

von Baltimore.

Baltimore,

Joh. Murphy & Co., 182 Marketstraße.

Zu haben in allen katholischen Buchhandlungen in den V. St

186·.

Bishop Neumann authored a catechism for German-speaking children.

the need to establish Catholic schools for every parish. The council urged each parish to set up a school without waiting for state help. It also was decided that a definitive catechism was necessary for religious instruction. Consequently, I was asked to write or choose a catechism for the German-speaking immigrant population. And so my own catechism became the one that was endorsed officially by the Council of Baltimore for German-speaking Catholics. I also was commissioned to write an official letter to the Leopoldine Foundation of Vienna to thank them for their generosity to German-speaking parishes and to urge their ongoing support. In addition, the council recommended the creation of eleven new dioceses. As a result, the New Jersey portion of my diocese became part of the Diocese of Newark. The council helped me in several ways. It allowed me to get acquainted with many of the bishops around the country, permitting me to see how my administrative challenges were like those in other dioceses. I believe that the council reached wise decisions, and I sought to incorporate all of them into the policies of my diocese.

When I returned to Philadelphia, the first subject I tackled was dear to my heart: the issue of Catholic schools. We held three meetings on the subject and adopted a central board of education for the Diocese of Philadelphia. We were charged with seeking funds for the expansion of schools throughout the diocese. In addition, the board was charged with recommending a general plan of instruction for local parish schools while the pastors continued to hire and pay salaries to the teachers. In my mind, it was important that the school be a separate building with its own space, equipment, and competent teachers to instruct the children. I was pleased with the development of the school system.

I was also concerned about the need for uniformity in worship, particularly since the Church in America represented so many different nationalities and customs. This concern was shared by the Plenary Council of Baltimore.

Not all my endeavors in the diocese were as successful as desired. I was unable to stimulate the construction progress of the cathedral in the manner I had hoped or in a way that some of my people expected. Financially, I took the same conservative approach I had taken as vicegerent of the Redemptorists and made the rule that the construction of the cathedral could progress only as rapidly as monies were collected. I wrote to the pastors, letting them know that it was their responsibility to solicit funds for the chair of the diocese. This was not a popular reminder—especially given all the urgent building needs in the individual parishes. The first drive raised only $5,000, and construction of the cathedral was almost suspended. The following year, I approached the subject at our diocesan synod. The pastors responded generously and decided to increase the contribution fourfold that year. I wrote a thank-you letter to the people for their generosity and had high hopes for the future.

Construction on the Cathedral of Sts. Peter and Paul was slow, but the many building programs in the parishes progressed. By the end of my second year as bishop, we had completed the construction of six churches begun before I came to Philadelphia. We also rebuilt six other churches and constructed thirty new ones for a total of forty-two parish facilities in thirty-four months. I set a goal of visiting every parish in the city of Philadelphia each year and every outlying parish every two years. While on these visits I examined parish books, checked financial records, heard confessions, confirmed parishioners, preached, and visited the sick. It was extremely tiring, but a wonderful part of my years serving as bishop. To meet this goal, I spent nearly half my time on the road performing these duties in the country districts. Some of the people in Philadelphia were none too happy about my absences and the attention I was paying to the rural parishes. Despite their chagrin, regular visits to all parishes remained my high priority.

In my early years as bishop, I panicked when the Vincentian superior general in Rome, due to a shortage of men, withdrew priests who were instructors from our diocesan seminary of St. Charles. My own priests were already so taxed, and I knew it was essential to provide good educators for our future clergy. It was also essential that we continued to have a seminary in the diocese. I asked Fr. William O'Hara from St. Patrick's Church to be the new superior of the seminary. Together, we recruited other capable clergymen to serve as professors. So, by the grace of God, we averted the tragedy of having to close the seminary, especially at a time when native clergy were so needed.

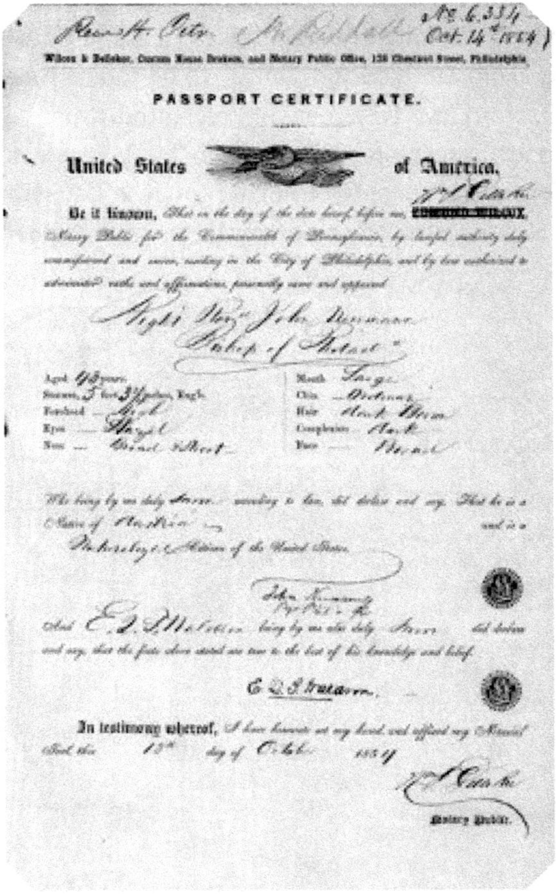
No. 6334 Oct. 14th 1854

PASSPORT CERTIFICATE.

United States of America.

Be it Known, That on the day of the date hereof, before me, [illegible] Notary Public for the Commonwealth of Pennsylvania, by lawful authority duly commissioned and sworn, residing in the City of Philadelphia, and by law authorized to administer oaths and affirmations, personally came and appeared

Right Rev. John Neumann
Bishop of Philadelphia

Aged 43 years, Stature, 5 feet 3½ inches, Eng. Forehead [illegible] Eyes Hazel Nose [illegible]

Mouth Large Chin [illegible] Hair Dark Brown Complexion Dark Face Round

Who being by me duly sworn according to law, did declare and say, That he is a Native of Austria and is a Naturalized Citizen of the United States.

John Neumann

And [illegible] being by me also duly sworn did declare and say, that the facts above stated are true to the best of his knowledge and belief.

In testimony whereof, I have hereunto set my hand and affixed my Notarial Seal this 13th day of October 1854

Notary Public.

Bishop Neumann's passport as an American citizen

CHAPTER 7

Return to Europe—
and to My Eternal Home

TOWARD THE END OF 1854, A WONDERFUL
EVENT WAS ANNOUNCED THAT FILLED MY
SOUL WITH GREAT JOY. The Holy Father, Pope Pius
IX, announced he was declaring the Immaculate Conception of Mary a dogma of the Catholic Church. I had always
honored our Lady under that title and was delighted with
Rome's decision. It also gave me the opportunity to make
my report concerning the Diocese of Philadelphia to the
Pope. This report required I travel to Rome. It would also
allow me the opportunity to visit my family in Europe after
an absence of nearly twenty years.

My journey across the Atlantic for the declaration of
the dogma was better than my first trip in 1836. Compared
to my original forty-day voyage, this one lasted only seventeen days, and I had privacy! I arrived in Le Havre and

crossed France by rail. In Marseilles, I boarded a small vessel for the port of Rome. For the two months I was in Rome, I was able to live in the Redemptorist community of Santa Maria in Monterone. There, I was able to live as a Redemptorist. I wore the habit every day rather than a bishop's regalia and attended all the community prayers. Private time with the Holy Father for my report was a deeply moving experience. I was scheduled to meet with him on December 16 to report on the situation in my diocese. My report elicited high praise from the Vatican officials. Being so close to the daily struggles of the diocese, I sometimes tended to overlook the obstacles I had already overcome during my time as bishop. I suppose I have always considered the daily effort of putting one foot in front of the other as nothing special. Nonetheless, others were more impressed and clearly saw the progress that had been made in the diocese.

While I had the ear of the Holy Father, I told him about my plans to start an orphanage for German immigrant children. Too often, they were either left without family, or they were temporarily abandoned by parents who had to focus on getting their feet on the ground. We already had two wonderful orphanages in the diocese, but we needed one that specifically served German children. I shared with him that I wanted to recruit sisters from the Third Order of St. Dominic to oversee this effort. Instead, the Pope suggested that I gather women from the United States to do the ministry I envisioned and then form them into a Third Order of St. Francis of Assisi. My mind began to race because, at that time, I knew of three women who were planning to form a religious community together at St. Peter's in Philadelphia. Pope Pius IX's counsel seemed so prophetic to me that I was able to meet with the Franciscan superior general in Rome, who then gave me permission to receive and profess members of the Third Order of St. Francis as sisters. From that blessed moment, a new community of dedicated sisters took root in my mind.

After spending time in Rome, I began my journey back home to Bohemia to visit family and friends. On January 30, I traveled to the beloved České Budějovice to visit my alma mater and the bishop there. He wanted me to take his carriage to Prachatice, but I asked that my arrival back home be quiet and secretive. My plan for a quiet return was not to be. As I neared Netolice outside of Prachatice, the church bells announced the arrival of the hometown boy who had made it big in America! People poured out of their houses to greet me and insisted I stay overnight in the small town. I had planned to walk home from there. The next morning, however, the magnificent sleigh of Prince Schwarzenberg was there to take me home. It had four horses and a coachman. People assembled along the entire way, ringing bells and welcoming me home with

Bishop Neumann supported establishing the Sisters of the Third Order of St. Francis, who began by serving in hospital ministry and developed into teaching schoolchildren.

signs depicting my bishop's coat of arms. I could not believe the fanfare and enthusiastic reception they gave me. I wondered to myself what they would think if they knew that some of the more sophisticated people of Philadelphia viewed me as unfit for the diocese.

When I got home, my eighty-year-old father embraced me and lifted me off the ground with a hug. He could only say time and again, "My son, my son!" For seven days, I stayed in my childhood home and said daily Mass in our beautiful parish church with a full congregation. I was only able to escape home without the fanfare of a glorious send-off by rising before dawn and leaving before anyone knew it was my day to depart. This was the second time I left home in secret. I just could not bear to do it any other way.

My visit to Europe was marvelous! I left the continent on the last day of February and made it back to the United States in seventeen days. The very night I returned to New York Harbor, I headed back to my home in Philadelphia. Two days later, I had dinner with the Redemptorists at St. Peter's, filled them in on all the confreres I saw in Europe, and told them about all the happenings in the Congregation around the world. It was a very pleasant visit. In May, I issued a second pastoral letter on the Immaculate Conception, praising the Mother of God and her glories. The grind of daily work quickly returned, and the European trip soon seemed like a distant memory.

Despite the bigotry against Catholics, the Church grew rapidly, and we did all we could to help Catholic immigrants. As I mentioned, while in Rome I told the Holy Father that I wanted to establish an orphanage for German children. I had to do what I could to help, so I undertook the building of an orphanage. The St. Vincent Orphan Society was established with help from the German pastors of St. Peter's, Holy Trinity, and St. Alphonsus parishes. Property was purchased, and construction of the orphanage began.

In our works of mercy, success was directly related to the tireless dedication of our women religious. The struggles these women endured as a result of deep poverty, the overwhelming needs of immigrants, and intimidation from some Americans was an inspiration to many women who desired to become a part of their ministry. This was a great blessing for the Church in the United States. As you can imagine, the Sisters of the Third Order of St. Francis were special. Although teaching would become part of the community's ministry, care of the sick was the root of their beginnings. I was able to be part of their history because of my position in the diocese and my interest in their religious life. I gave conferences to them on the duties of the religious life and was diligent in establishing the new community on a solid foundation by providing them with a rule written by my own hand. The lives of these women were austere and penitential, and spiritual happiness radiated from them.

I had occasion to visit other women religious, and it was always a joy to be with them. On another occasion, I visited the Sisters of St. Joseph. These women lived in great poverty—so much so that they often lacked enough food to eat or enough coal for the fire to heat their house. It was customary for me to give religious medals to the sisters after our meetings together. This time, however, I gave them "Yankee medals"—fifty dollars in gold pieces to help them survive their winter crisis.

The diocesan pastors were central to the life of the local parishes. I made myself available whenever it was convenient for them to visit and urged that they continue their dedicated apostolic work.

Managing a diocese the size of Philadelphia's was challenging. To ease the strain, I proposed that the diocese be divided in two—one covering the metropolitan area of Philadelphia and the other for the surrounding countryside. I proposed that I take over the portion that covered the countryside. It seemed to me that I would be better suited for that rural territory while a more sophisticated bishop could serve the metropolitan area. Unfortunately, the mechanisms of the Church were not that simple. It was difficult for Church officials in Rome to imagine why a bishop in a prestigious diocese like Philadelphia would want to move to a lesser diocese. They were certain that the press would attempt to find a reason for my "demotion"—even if I insisted that it was my idea to make such a move. Rather than instituting my suggestion, a coadjutor bishop with the right of succession, James Wood, was sent to help me. Once on board in the diocese as coadjutor, it soon was apparent that he thought he would be moving into my role upon my resignation—which was not going to happen. He thought I would remain in Philadelphia only long enough for me to transfer all the properties of the diocese from my name to his so he could then take over. But I never had any intention of resigning from being a bishop. I only wished to take a smaller role in the diocese. I asked Bishop Wood to assume oversight of the finances of the diocese, and he did a marvelous job. He had worked in finance before entering the ministry and was suited for the task. I tried not to interfere too often—or at least not in a manner that would embarrass him. Nevertheless, we had our differences of opinion.

In the fall of 1859, we opened the preparatory seminary at Glen Riddle with four professors and twenty-six young students. I was delighted. I was hopeful about the institution and what it would mean for the future of the diocese. Of equal importance to the future of the diocese was the establishment of the Sisters of the Servants of the Immaculate Heart of Mary. Mother Theresa Maxis Duchemin was a dynamo and had definite ideas about the way things should happen. She wrote to let me know that the sisters

Bishop Neumann spurred construction of the Cathedral of Sts. Peter and Paul in Philadelphia.

were available to minister in the diocese. An opportunity for this possibility soon presented itself. Fr. John Vincent O'Reilly in Susquehanna County found himself with an empty academy when the Sisters of the Holy Cross withdrew. Fr. O'Reilly contacted the Sisters of the Servants of the Immaculate Heart of Mary in Monroe, Michigan, to help with this work. They were growing in number and were looking for a place to expand their ministry. In addition, having a Redemptorist bishop was thought an advantage to these sisters, who list a Redemptorist as their founder. When Fr. O'Reilly asked me what I thought about this arrangement, I gave him a favorable reply. I was always interested in establishing solid educational institutions.

Meanwhile, the slow progress on the construction of the cathedral was a complicated issue and a constant thorn in my side. Finally, on September 14, 1859, the feast of the Exaltation of the Holy Cross, we completed the exterior of the building and were finally ready to place the gold cross atop the dome. It was a long time in coming, and much work still needed to be done to complete the project. While we were only finished with the exterior, it was a marvelous milestone. Six thousand people joined us in Logan Square for the occasion to watch the eleven-foot cross lifted to the rooftop. I asked Bishop Wood to be the celebrant for the ceremony, and he gladly accepted. I assisted, content enough to have completed this part of the task.

I was in Philadelphia for Christmas in 1859. I heard many confessions and pontificated at the Midnight Mass at St. Peter the Apostle Church. It was splendid to celebrate the birth of our Lord with such a wonderfully large and devout congregation. After walking back home from St. Peter's, I said my second Christmas Mass in private, recalling the silence of the stable in Bethlehem. I then celebrated the ten o'clock Mass at St. John the Evangelist, the protocathedral. After Christmas, I had much desk work to complete. I was pleasantly surprised when a friend came to visit from Buffalo and updated me about so many of my former parishioners. Days later, another priest, Fr. Anthony Urbanczik, stopped by for a visit. I must not have looked too well and, after he commented on my appearance, I told him: "I have a strange feeling today," I said. "I feel as I never felt before. I have to go out on a little business, and the fresh air will do me good. A man must always be ready, for death comes when and where God wills it."

I had to visit a lawyer about a property deed, and I also had to check on a chalice that was sent to Fr. Otto Kopf but seemed to have gotten lost in transit. On that errand, at Vine Street near Thirteenth, I met my end. I died in the parlor of a Protestant gentleman after collapsing on his stoop. I would have preferred to have been surrounded by my confreres and to exit this world amid the Divine Office. Instead, I died with a simple sigh that committed my soul into the hands of my Savior. I was forty-eight years old when I died of apoplexy, left this world, and entered eternal life.

I never seemed to be able to enter places quietly. When I returned to Prachatice, it seemed that everyone turned out to welcome me. Similarly, I do not know where the people came from on the day of my funeral. Logan Square was packed when they carried my remains from the bishop's chapel to St. John's for the first funeral Mass, and then again as we processed to St. Peter the Apostle. The police and a brass band led the procession, which included a rifle company, various societies and sodalities, my dear seminarians, fifty or so prelates, and hundreds of priests, religious, and laity of the diocese. I could not believe how many people came to pay their respects!

You never would have guessed that anyone had ever said a word against me if you would have heard the outpouring at my funeral. In fact, I was beginning to wonder if I would ever be laid to rest in my grave! I had made it known that I wanted to be buried among my confreres, so I was pleased when Fr. John De Dyker, the provincial, asked to have me buried at St. Peter the Apostle. Bishop Wood left the decision to Archbishop Kenrick, who gladly consented and was content that I would at last be able to rest among my confreres. I am now at peace, buried among my confreres in the chapel of the parish church.

"I have a strange feeling today," I said. "I feel as I never felt before. I have to go out on a little business, and the fresh air will do me good. A man must always be ready, for death comes when and where God wills it."

A rare portrait of Fr. John Neumann in his Redemptorist habit

Prayers for St. John Neumann's Intercession

Let us pray together: Oh my Jesus, how I glory in belonging to you! Draw me powerfully to your holy cross, that I, too, may become pure, and pious, and holy. Jesus, searcher of hearts, you know how mine longs to be holy, to be united with you! Your death, Jesus, made all people my brothers and sisters! Come, then, Holy Spirit, come upon me that I may show forth to your world the way of eternal salvation! Come upon me, strength of the weak, that my life and my works may exhibit faith made fruitful by your grace! Holy Spirit, direct me in all my ways! With the Blessed Virgin, your Mother, and with St. Joseph, I kneel at your crib and weep over my sins but ask again your grace. You are my all, my Lord, my God!

Oh my Jesus, how I glory in belonging to you! Draw me powerfully to your holy cross, that I, too, may become pure and pious and holy. Jesus, searcher of hearts, you know how mine longs to be holy, to be united with you! Your death, Jesus, made all people my brothers and sisters! Come, then, Holy Spirit, come upon me that I may show forth to your world the way of eternal salvation! Come upon me, strength of the weak, that my life and my works may exhibit faith made fruitful by your grace! Holy Spirit, direct me in all my ways! With the Blessed Virgin, your Mother, and with St. Joseph, I kneel at your crib and weep over my sins but ask again your grace. You are my all, my Lord, my God!

Saint John Neumann's prayer for holiness at the time of his ordination

Sing praise to St. John Neumann
In every age and place
Who brought to all who knew him
The comfort of God's grace.

Saint John Neumann, faithful pastor of your congregations, we come to you now with our difficulties. As you
always made yourself available to your parishioners when
you were in our world, we are confident you will hear our
prayer. We ask you to join us in storming heaven for our
need. We know the goodness of God and ask you to join
us in our petitions today.

Pray for our special intentions of this day.

We turn to St. John Neumann
With hope in every need!
He stands before the Father
The cause of all to plead.

Saint John Neumann, one of your first concerns in your pastoral ministry was always the children. You established the Catholic school system from your concern that the teachings of the Church and the freedom to study the arts and sciences without prejudice was possible, free of the prejudice so often visited upon the children because of their religion. Take care of the children in my family and all those I know of who are in special need of your help. We trust your concern and know you will join us in our prayers.

Pray for the children you know who are in special need.

We thank you St. John Neumann
And through this poem we pray
To share in all God's graces
And live with Him one day.

Saint John Neumann, remember those who have recently arrived in our country. You served so faithfully the immigrants of your day in all their needs. Bless the many generous souls who serve the most needy in our country. Never let us be blind to their needs and inspire us to do our part to help them as well.

Pray for the poor who are struggling in our midst.

Saint John Neumann, when you established the Forty Hours devotion in your diocese, you showed your great love for our Lord in the holy Eucharist. Give us that same love of Jesus Christ present with us. By the grace of your journey to Rome for the solemn declaration of the Immaculate Conception of Mary, let us always honor and serve the Blessed Virgin. By your welcoming and gathering of religious around you, inspire us to encourage vocations to the religious life so that the needs of the people will be served in so many ways.

Pray for the needs of the Church today.

Saint John Neumann, we bring to you the needs of our world and our own personal needs with a great assurance that you will hear our prayer and join us in presenting our petitions to God. As you have helped so many people while you were here, stay with us today and bless us and our efforts to remain steadfast in our faith.

Hear our prayer, we ask of you
Be with us in all we do!
Comfort us, strengthen us,
Keep us close to God and you.

Saint John Neumann, pray for us. Amen.

For Further Reading

Archival Sources

American Catholic Historical Society (AMCHS.org).

Redemptorist Archives of the Baltimore Province: Neu-manniana (Redemptorists.net).

Printed Sources

Acta Apostolicae Sedis (Vatican.va).

Archdiocese of Philadelphia (Archphila.org).

Spicilegium Historicum Congregationis SSmi. Redemptoris

Books

Berger, Johann, CSsR, *Life of the Right Rev. John N. Neumann*. Translated by Eugene Grimm, CSsR, Philadelphia, 1884.

Boever, Richard A. CSsR, *Saint John Neumann: His Writings and Spirituality*. Liguori, Missouri, 2010.

Boever, Richard A., CSsR, *The Spirituality of St. John Neumann, CSsR, Fourth Bishop of Philadelphia*. Ann Arbor, Michigan; University Microfilms International, 1983.

Chorpenning, Joseph F., OSFS, ed. *He Spared Himself in Nothing: Essays on the Life and Thought of John Nepomucene Neumann*. Philadelphia, 2003.

Curley, Michael J, CSsR, *Venerable John Neumann, CSsR*. Washington, 1952.

Dolan, Jay P. *The Immigrant Church*. Notre Dame, 1978.

Light, Dale B. *Rome and the New Republic*. Notre Dame, 1966.

Neumann, John N., CSsR, *Bublische Geschichte des Alten und Neuen Testamentes*. Baltimore, 1849.

———. *Katholischer Katechismus*. Pittsburgh, 1846.

———. *Manuale Devotionis Quadraginta Horarum*. Philadelphia, 1855.

Rush, Alfred C., CSsR, ed. *The Autobiography of St. John Neumann*. Boston, 1977.

Wuest, Joseph, CSsR. *Annales Provinciae Americanae*. Ilchester, Maryland, 1888.

About the Author

Fr. Richard Boever, CSsR, PhD, has been in the Catholic ministry since 1974. He served as a parish priest and pastor in St. Louis and Chicago, taught theology at Newman University and Saint Louis University, served as a university chaplain, and he has been the director of Redemptorist formation for the prenovitiate program. He also held various positions at Liguori Publications, including president and publisher. He was a retreat director in Oconomowoc, Wisconsin, and served as a research expert at the Neumann Shrine in Philadelphia. Fr. Rich currently is the executive director at the National Shrine of Blessed Francis Xavier Seelos in New Orleans. He has authored many books for Liguori Publications, including *The 5W's of the Catholic Faith: Living in Hope* (2012) and *Zealous Missionary: From the Perspective of Blessed Francis Xavier Seelos* (2021).

The National Shrine of St. John Neumann
The shrine and its website are designed to familiarize people with the shrine's ministry and with St. John Neumann, the first male saint of the United States, who continues to inspire the work of the shrine daily.

"St. John Neumann was a tireless preacher of the gospel to the most abandoned, especially the poor," says the website. "At his shrine, we strive to imitate his example, welcoming all who come to visit his tomb and offering pilgrims a respite from the busy streets of the city for prayer, worship, reconciliation, and renewal."

You are invited to explore the shrine, its website, and all of the resources noted in this book to discover the grace offered to the Church and the world through the man known as Philadelphia's "Little Bishop," St. John Neumann, CSsR.

The National Shrine of St. John Neumann
1019 North Fifth Street
Philadelphia, Pennsylvania 19123
(215) 627-3080
stjohnneumann.org